**W9-ATF-106**

DATE DUE

Managing Our Resources

Rocks
A resource our world depends on

Heinemann Library
Chicago, Illinois

Ian Graham

552
Gra
c.1 2007
28.21

Designed by David Poole and
Paul Myerscough
Photo research by Melissa Allison and
Andrea Sadler

Originated by Ambassador Litho Ltd.
Printed in China by WKT Company Limited

09 08 07 06 05

10 9 8 7 6 5 4 3 2 1

**Library of Congress Cataloging-in-
Publication Data**
Graham, Ian, 1953-
  Rocks : a resource our world depends on /
Ian Graham.
     p. cm. -- (Managing our resources)
  Includes bibliographical references and
index.
  ISBN 1-4034-5617-8 (lib. bdg.) --
  ISBN 1-4034-5625-9 (pbk.)
  1. Rocks--Juvenile literature. I. Title. II.
Series.
  QE432.2.G7 2005
  552--dc22
                                    2004005908

Acknowledgments
The author and publisher are grateful to the
following for permission to reproduce
copyright material: p. 4 Dave
Johnson/Harcourt Education Ltd.; p. 5
bottom Maurice Nimmo/FLPA; p. 5 top
Maurice Nimmo/FLPA; p. 6 Peter
Evans/Harcourt Education Ltd.; pp. 7, 9, 19
bottom Photodisc/Getty Images; p. 8
Construction Photography; p. 10 Visual
Image/Harcourt Education Ltd.; pp. 12, 24
top, 24 bottom, 26, 27 NOAA; pp. 13, 22
(Barnabas Bosshart) Corbis; p. 14 David
Hosking/FLPA; pp. 15, 19 top, 21 QA Photos;
p. 16 Peter Hulme/Ecoscene; pp. 17 A.
Comu/Publiphoto Diffusion/Science Photo
Library; p. 18 Bridgeman Art Library; p. 20
top ImageWorks/Topham Picturepoint; p. 20
bottom NASA/Science Photo Library; p. 23
Charles E. Rotkin/Corbis; p. 25
Bettmann/Corbis; p. 28 top Anthony
Cooper/Ecoscene; p. 28 bottom Tony
Hamblin FRPS/Ecoscene; p. 29 Corbis.

Cover photograph: Hans Georg Roth/Corbis.

Every effort has been made to contact
copyright holders of any material
reproduced in this book. Any omissions will
be rectified in subsequent printings if notice
is given to the publisher.

Contents

Some words are shown in bold, **like this.** You can find out what they mean by looking in the glossary.

What Is Rock?

Rock is a natural resource found in the ground. There are different kinds of rocks. Some are light, some are heavy, some are soft, and some are hard. Rocks are often different colors because they contain different mixtures of **minerals.** Minerals are made from tiny crystals. These are like grains of salt that are joined together.

There are three main types of rock—igneous, sedimentary, and metamorphic. Each type of rock is formed in a different way.

Igneous rock

Igneous rock is made when hot, liquid rock, called **magma** or **lava,** cools down and becomes solid. Igneous means fiery. Basalt and **granite** are examples of igneous rock.

This is granite, an igneous rock. You can see the crystals of different minerals that make up the rock.

Sedimentary rock

Frost, wind, the Sun's heat, and other forces of nature break down rock into smaller and smaller pieces. Eventually they are as small as grains of **sand**. Rain washes them into rivers and the sea, where they sink to the bottom. In this form, they are known as sediment. The weight of more and more material piling up on top of them presses the **particles** together so tightly that they form rock. Sandstone is one example of sedimentary rock.

Sandstone is a sedimentary rock. You can see the grains of sand and other particles that have been pressed together to make the rock.

Metamorphic rock

Rock is sometimes heated or pressed together so much that it changes into a new type of rock, called metamorphic rock. *Metamorphic* is a word that means "changed." **Marble** is one example of metamorphic rock. It starts as a chalky sedimentary rock called **limestone**. Then heat from hot rock underground and the weight of earth and water above pressing down change it into marble.

Marble is a metamorphic rock. It usually contains colored swirls and veins made from different minerals.

What Is Rock Used For?

You can see rock all around you. It is in your home and your streets. Some types of rock are very hard and last for a long time. This makes rock ideal as a building material. When rock is taken from nature and used for a purpose, such as building, it is called stone. Thousands of years ago, ancient peoples made their most important buildings from stone. Some of them still exist today because they were made from this hard, long-lasting material. The Great Pyramid of Khufu near Giza, Egypt, was built 4,500 years ago. It contains 2.3 million massive stones. Stone was chosen as the best material to protect the tomb of the Egyptian king who was buried inside the pyramid.

It took thousands of people twenty years to build Egypt's Great Pyramid.

Did you know?

When the pyramids at Giza, Egypt, were built, they were covered with smooth, white **limestone**. Most of the limestone is now gone. It either fell away or was stolen and used in other buildings.

How is rock used for building today?

Today, crushed rock is used in the foundations, or the deepest layers, of roads and buildings. More expensive types of stone, such as **marble,** are sometimes used to make the walls of fancy buildings.

Why do people go to mountains?

Mountains are giant piles of rock that tower over the surrounding land. Today, tourists visit mountains to look at them and photograph them. Mountaineers climb them. In ancient times, people were attracted to mountains for different reasons. Some people worshiped them as gods. Others thought that gods lived on the snow-capped, cloud-covered mountaintops.

Gravestones are made of stone so that they last for a very long time.

Did you know?

The ancient Greek people believed that Mount Olympus was the home of gods. The Maori people of New Zealand call the country's tallest mountain Aoraki. In their legends, Aoraki was a son of the Sky Father who was turned into rock.

How is rock used to clean things?

Some cleaning products contain fine, powdered rock. When it is rubbed over something, the rough **particles** wear away dirt and grime on the surface. One way of cleaning stone buildings, called sandblasting, makes use of rock particles, too. Grains of sand or a similar material are blown down a hose by a jet of air. They fly out and hit the stone. They act like millions of tiny hammers, beating away all of the dirt and cleaning the stone.

How is rock used in sports?

Heavy stones were used for weightlifting competitions in the past. Today, the sport of curling still uses stones. Two teams slide heavy stones along ice so that the stones stop as close as possible to a target, called the tee or button.

Dirt, grime, and soot that builds up on stone buildings over many years can be cleaned off by sandblasting.

CASE STUDY:
Mount Rushmore

One of the biggest and most impressive **monuments** made from rock anywhere in the world is Mount Rushmore National **Memorial** in South Dakota. It is a **sculpture** of four heads, each about 60 feet (18 meters) high, in the side of a mountain. They are the heads of four United States presidents—George Washington, Thomas Jefferson, Theodore Roosevelt, and Abraham Lincoln. Explosives were used to blast 50,000 tons of rock away. Then, workers hanging from cables used hammers and drills to carve away the rest of the rock. The **granite** was so hard that drills had to be resharpened after only 18 inches (45 centimeters) of drilling. The work began in 1927 and finished in 1941.

The four heads of the Mount Rushmore National Memorial are carved out of a mountain.

Where Is Rock Found?

Rock is found all over Earth and also inside it. The surface of Earth is made from rock. In many places, it is covered with soil or water, but if you dig down far enough, you will reach rock. But Earth is not solid rock all the way through. The rock at the surface is called the **crust**. Underneath the crust, there is a layer about 1,810 miles (2,900 kilometers) deep that is called the mantle. The rock the mantle is made from, called **magma,** is so hot that it flows slowly, like thick syrup. At the center of Earth, there is a ball-shaped **core** about 4,350 miles (7,000 kilometers) across. It is made mainly from iron. The center of the core is solid, but the outside part is liquid.

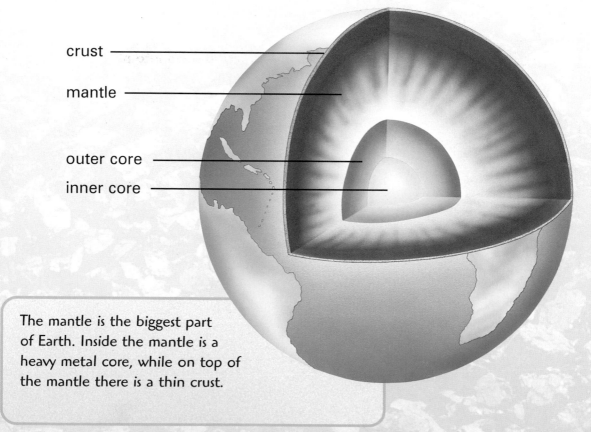

crust

mantle

outer core

inner core

The mantle is the biggest part of Earth. Inside the mantle is a heavy metal core, while on top of the mantle there is a thin crust.

What is Earth's crust like?

Earth's crust is not a solid shell of rock. It is made up of pieces, called plates, like a cracked eggshell. The plates move slowly in different directions. In places where they push against each other, there are earthquakes and **volcanoes**. Underneath the oceans, some plates are moving apart. Molten, or melted, rock rises up into the gap between them and cools to form solid rock.

How thick is Earth's crust?

Earth's crust is thinnest under the middle parts of the oceans. There, it is as little as 4 miles (6 kilometers) thick. The rest of the crust is much thicker—up to about 44 miles (70 kilometers) thick.

Earth's crust is divided into plates of rock.

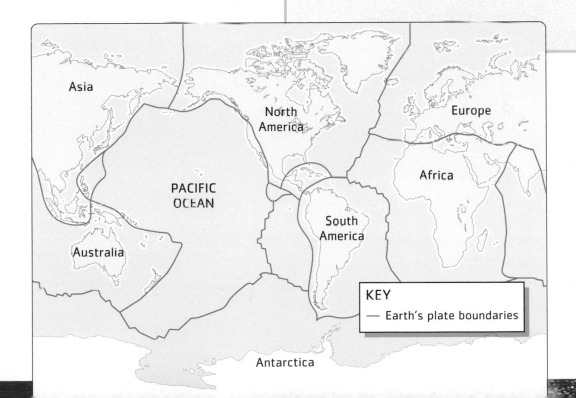

Asia

North America

Europe

Africa

PACIFIC OCEAN

South America

Australia

KEY

— Earth's plate boundaries

Antarctica

11

How does Earth's crust move?

The smoke from a fire floats upward because hot air rises. Very hot rock inside Earth rises, too, but much more slowly. Heat from the center of Earth makes **magma** rise up through the mantle. As the magma rises, it cools and sinks down again. These slow-moving currents in the mantle make the **crust** on top of it move, too.

The forces that move Earth's crust are enormous. They are strong enough to bend or break the rocky crust. If the rock is hot enough and pushed slowly enough, it folds. If the rock is colder, more brittle, and is pushed too quickly, it breaks. A break in Earth's crust is called a fault.

Did you know?

The oldest of Earth's rocks found so far are 4 billion years old. They were found in Canada.

The San Andreas fault, where two of the world's great crust plates meet, runs through the state of California.

CASE STUDY:
Mount Everest

The tallest mountain on Earth is Mount Everest. It is located in the Himalayan mountain range on the border between Nepal and China. Its summit, or highest point, stands 29,035 feet (8,850 meters) above sea level. It was climbed for the first time in 1953. Two climbers named Edmund Hilary and Tenzing Norgay reached its summit.

The Himalayas lie along the line where two plates of Earth's crust meet. The plate with India on top is pushing northward into the plate that Europe and Asia sit on. They met 50 million years ago. As one plate pushed into the other, the ground was forced upward to form the mountains. About half a million years ago, they became the tallest mountains on Earth.

Mount Everest was found to be the tallest mountain on Earth in 1852.

CASE STUDY:
Uluru (Ayers Rock), Australia

Uluru is one of the most famous pieces of rock on Earth. It used to be known as Ayers Rock. It rises to a height of 1,100 feet (335 meters) above the surrounding desert in Australia's Northern Territory. It measures 2.2 miles (3.6 kilometers) long by 1.2 miles (2 kilometers) wide. Although it looks huge, it is just the tip of a mountain that stood on an ocean floor 500 million years ago. Then, movements in Earth's **crust** pushed the ocean floor upward. Today, Uluru's base is buried about four miles (6 kilometers) below the ground and only the very top can be seen. It is a sacred place for Aborigines, Australia's native people, who believe it is home to spirits of beings from their history.

Uluru in Australia appears to turn a deep red-orange color in the morning and evening, when the Sun is low in the sky. Uluru is made of a rock called arkose, a type of sandstone.

How Is Rock Processed?

Rock is **processed** in many different ways. It may simply be washed before it is used. If the pieces are too big, they are crushed and sorted into different sizes. Rock can be heated and mixed with other materials to **extract** metals, such as iron. **Limestone** is used to make cement, which is used to make concrete.

What is concrete?

Concrete is a mixture of sand, cement, water, and small pieces of rock called gravel. Concrete can be poured and shaped when it is freshly mixed. It then sets as hard as rock.

Did you know?

The ancient Romans made cement more than 2,000 years ago. It is also known as *pozzolana* because it contained volcanic ash found near the town of Pozzuoli.

This vehicle was used to crush rock during the construction of the Channel Tunnel between England and France.

Why are some rocks called ores?

Rocks are made from thousands of different **minerals**. About 100 of these minerals contain useful materials, mainly metals. These minerals are called **ore** minerals, or ores. Small amounts of pure metals—such as gold, copper, and tin—are found in the ground, but most metals have to be **extracted** from ores. Iron comes from several different ores, including hematite and magnetite. Tin comes from an ore called cassiterite.

How do we get metal from rock?

In nature, ores are usually mixed together with other types of rock in the ground. Each ore has to be separated from the unwanted rock.

Rock is dug out of the ground at places called **quarries.**

Then the metal is extracted from the ore. This is done through a **process** called smelting. Smelting works by heating an ore inside a furnace to such a high temperature that the metal melts and runs out. As it cools, it changes from a liquid into solid metal.

How hot does the furnace have to be?

Different metals melt at different temperatures. A furnace has to be hot enough to melt the metal, so the temperature of a furnace depends on which metal it is producing. Copper melts at 1,981 °F (1,083 °C), but iron does not melt until it reaches a temperature of 2,795 °F (1,535 °C).

Metals are produced by smelting ores in furnaces.

Did you know?

People first obtained copper by the process of smelting about 7,000 years ago.

How long have people used rock?

People have made things from rock for more than two million years. **Stone Age** people made axes and other tools out of rock. Ancient people also carved and painted rock. We know a lot about ancient Egypt because many of its stone buildings and **monuments** are covered with paintings and carvings that tell stories of its people and their history. Today, stone statues and other **sculptures** in public places mark important events and people in our history.

What did prehistoric people use flint for?

Stone Age people used all kinds of rock, but a rock called flint was especially useful. When a piece of flint is hit in the right way, razor-sharp flakes fly off it. These flakes made excellent cutting tools.

The statue of David was made from a block of **marble** 500 years ago by the Italian artist Michelangelo.

How Do Scientists Use Rocks?

Scientists who study rocks are called **geologists.** Geologists use rocks to learn more about Earth and what has happened to it since it formed about 4.6 billion years ago. They also study rocks to find valuable materials such as oil, gold, and other metals. Rocks contain a record of the history of Earth and the plants and animals that have lived on it.

Geologists collect rock samples and take them back to their laboratory to study.

How do rocks record life on Earth?

When animals that lived millions of years ago died, their soft parts rotted away quickly, leaving bones, teeth, and shells. If they died in water, they were soon covered with mud. In time, water rich in **minerals** soaked through the bones and changed them into **fossils.**

Some rocks contain fossils, the remains of plants and animals that died a long time ago.

What have we learned about the Moon by studying rocks?

Twelve American astronauts who landed on the Moon brought 840 pounds (380 kilograms) of moon rocks back to Earth with them. By studying these rocks, scientists have learned more about how the Moon was formed. Scientists believe Earth was hit by an object the size of a planet like Mars. It blasted rock out of Earth's surface into space. All of the millions of pieces of rock slowly came together to form the Moon. Spacecraft are still being sent to the Moon and the planets to study them.

The Mars *Pathfinder* space mission landed the *Sojourner* rover vehicle on the surface of the planet Mars in 1997. It moved around and studied rocks on the planet's surface.

Do scientists study other space rocks?

When the Sun and planets formed, many pieces of rock were left over. Many of them are still flying through space today. A few hit Earth every year. They are called meteorites. **Geologists** collect meteorites and study them.

Meteorites are rocks from space that land on Earth.

CASE STUDY:
The Channel Tunnel

In 1994 the Channel Tunnel opened after almost seven years of work. The tunnel lies under the sea between England and France. Before tunneling could begin, **geologists** had to find out what sort of rock lay beneath the seabed. They found several different layers of rock. One layer was chalk marl, which is a mixture of chalk and a type of soil called clay. It is a soft, waterproof rock, making it ideal for digging tunnels under the sea.

Giant machines tunneled through the rock. Each machine wedged itself in the tunnel and cutters on the front carved away the rock. Then the whole machine was pushed forward to cut more rock away. It cut through as much as 245 feet (75 meters) of rock every day.

Tunneling machines dug all the way from England to France underneath the English Channel.

How Is Rock Moved?

Rock is hard to move because of its great weight. Trucks haul rock out of **quarries** and mines. Trains and ships transport it over greater distances. The ships are called bulk carriers. Special bulk carriers called **ore** carriers are used for the heaviest loads. About 5,000 bulk carrier ships carry **cargoes** such as iron ore around the world. The biggest ore carriers can each transport more than 300,000 tons of ore.

Rock and ore are transported long distances by ships and trains. This train is transporting iron ore.

How did people move rock without modern machines?

People in the ancient world moved very big blocks of rock without the powerful machines we have today. About 5,000 years ago in England, people began to build a **monument** called Stonehenge. Over the next 1,000 years, circles of giant stones were added to it. The first 80 stones weighed more than four tons each.

Then, 30 more stones weighing up to 50 tons each were added. That is the same weight as about 30 cars! The stones were moved on water using wooden rafts whenever possible. On land, they were probably dragged on sleds or pushed along on top of logs that acted as rollers.

How is rock transported by road today?

The trucks used to transport rock in quarries and mines are giant vehicles. They are far too big to travel on ordinary roads. Rock is transported by road in tipper trucks. These trucks have a cargo tank at the back that can be tipped up. When the front end of the tank is raised, the back opens and the load slides out onto the ground.

Giant machines dig rock out of the ground. The rock is then loaded into tipper trucks like the one on the right.

How Can Rock Be Dangerous?

Rock is dangerous when it falls or flies through the air because it is so heavy. Falling rocks can block roads and hurt climbers. Rockfalls in mines can block tunnels and trap miners. **Volcanoes** can throw out enough rock and ash to bury a whole town. Earthquakes crack the ground open and cause dangerous rock slides.

Rock slides can block roads and bury buildings.

Radiation

Rock can be dangerous because of what it contains. Some substances give out harmful **particles** or rays of energy called radiation. Rocks that contain uranium give out a gas called radon and radon gives out radiation. The gas can collect in houses built on top of the rock. Breathing in too much radon for a long time can be bad for a person's health. Houses at risk are often fitted with air pumps to blow the gas away.

Did you know?

There are about twenty serious earthquakes every year. Some earthquakes are powerful enough to make buildings collapse.

CASE STUDY:
The Vaiont Dam Landslide, Italy

One of the biggest dams in the world was built across the Vaiont River in Italy in 1961. In 1963 a giant wall of water swept down the valley below the dam and drowned 2,500 people. Experts thought the dam must have burst, but they were amazed to see that it was still there.

The rock on each side of the valley had a layer of clay running through it. The water behind the dam stopped water in the valley walls from draining away. The water made the clay so slippery that the rock above it slid off. Millions of tons of rock fell into the **reservoir,** creating a giant wave. The wave then spilled over the top of the dam into the valley below.

The Vaiont Dam disaster was caused by a huge rock slide.

Why Are Volcanoes Dangerous?

When a **volcano** erupts, it throws out rock that has melted and turned into a liquid. This liquid rock is called **lava.** When the hot lava cools, it turns into a type of rock called basalt. Volcanoes can erupt in different ways. Sometimes lava pours out and flows down the sides of a volcano like a river of fire. Sometimes the lava explodes out of a volcano with enormous force, hurling huge rocks high into the air.

Volcanoes that erupt are called active volcanoes. Volcanoes that have not erupted for a long time are called dormant.

Did you know?

There are about 500 active volcanoes in the world today.

Volcanoes can erupt with a fiery explosion of hot lava. This is the Kilauea volcano in Hawaii.

CASE STUDY:
Mount Saint Helens

The biggest rock slide in recorded history happened in the United States. A volcano called Mount Saint Helens had not erupted for 123 years. Then, in 1980, the ground shook and a large bulge appeared on one side of the mountain. The bulge was **magma** rising up inside the mountain. On May 18, the whole bulging side of the mountain slid away and the magma underneath it exploded out. The top 1,312 feet (400 meters) of the mountain disappeared in just a few seconds. Snow and ice from the mountaintop melted and formed rivers. These raging torrents carried thousands of tons of loose rocks down the mountainside. Mount Saint Helens continued erupting for six years. When all the rocks came to rest and the lava cooled, the mountain and the land all around it had changed forever.

In 1980 Mount Saint Helens erupted. The magma that poured out flattened forests, killed 57 people and thousands of animals, and damaged 27 bridges and about 200 homes.

How Can We Protect the Environment?

Digging rock out of the ground creates ugly scars in the land and damages natural **habitats**. Rock is usually hauled away in big trucks. The noise, dust, and heavy traffic can be a nuisance to people living nearby. When a **quarry** or a mine closes, the site is often left to return to nature by itself. Sometimes people try to speed this up by covering the ground with new soil and plants.

Although closed quarries or mines can look natural again after they have been landscaped, it can take many, many years.

Digging up limestone

Limestone pavement is a rare type of rock formation that can be up to 300 million years old. Some limestone pavements have been destroyed to supply rock for landscaping.

Some limestone pavements have been destroyed by quarrying.

Will Rock Ever Run Out?

We will never run out of rock. New rock is constantly being formed by natural **processes** inside Earth. **Volcanoes** bring new rock up to the surface constantly.

Using stone again

In ancient times, people often took materials from old buildings and walls and used them for new buildings. When a wall collapsed or a building was left empty, the stones it was built from were carried away and used again. This still happens today. When old buildings are knocked down, the materials are sorted into bricks, stone blocks, roof tiles, wooden beams, flooring, and other materials that can be used again.

The Hawaiian islands in the Pacific Ocean are the tips of volcanoes. As more volcanoes erupt, more new land will be formed.

Glossary

cargo goods or materials transported in a vehicle, especially in large amounts

core central part of Earth or another body in space

crust rock that forms the surface of Earth

extract take something out of something else, such as coal out of a field

fossil remains of a plant or animal that lived many years ago

geologist scientist who studies rocks and minerals

granite type of igneous rock that is grey, very hard, and commonly used for building

habitat natural home of a plant or animal

lava melted rock produced by volcanoes

limestone chalky sedimentary rock formed from animal remains

magma melted rock in the mantle, the layer underneath Earth's crust

marble type of metamorphic rock. It usually contains colored swirls and veins made from different minerals.

memorial something by which the memory of a person or event is kept alive

mineral naturally occurring, solid substance that rocks are made of. Most minerals are made up from two or more substances combined.

monument statue, building, gravestone, or other object that is created to honor the memory of someone or something

ore mineral that is mined to obtain a substance, such as gold, that it contains

particle very small bit of something

process to change a material by a series of actions or treatments or the method by which a material is changed

quarry hole in the ground where building materials such as stone or gravel are dug out

reservoir place where something, such as water, is kept for use in the future

sculpture work of art made by carving or chiseling stone or wood, by modeling clay, or by pouring melted metal into a cast

Stone Age oldest time in history when people existed and made tools from stone. It started about 700,000 years ago. It lasted until about 4,000–5,000 years ago.

volcano vent, or hole, in Earth's crust from which melted or hot rock and steam come out

More Books to Read

O'Donoghue, Michael. *Rocks & Minerals of the World.* Chicago: World Book, 2004.

Stewart, Melissa. *Fossils.* Chicago: Heinemann Library, 2002.

Stewart, Melissa. *Igneous Rocks.* Chicago: Heinemann Library, 2002.

Stewart, Melissa. *Metamorphic Rocks.* Chicago: Heinemann Library, 2002.

Stewart, Melissa. *Minerals.* Chicago: Heinemann Library, 2002.

Stewart, Melissa. *Sedimentary Rocks.* Heinemann Library, 2002.

Whyman, Kathryn. *Rocks and Minerals and the Environment.* Mankato, Minn.: Stargazer Books, 2004.

Zemlicka, Shannon. *From Rock to Road.* Minneapolis, Minn.: Stargazer Books, 2004.

Index